Original title:
The Belt of Courage

Copyright © 2025 Creative Arts Management OÜ
All rights reserved.

Author: Ryan Sterling
ISBN HARDBACK: 978-1-80586-061-7
ISBN PAPERBACK: 978-1-80586-533-9

Threads that Stand Tall

In a world where socks just disappear,
A brave pair marches, full of cheer.
With patterns bold, and colors bright,
They tackle laundry with all their might.

They tie their laces double tight,
And dance around, what a sight!
With buttons shiny, and seams so fine,
They strut their stuff, feeling divine.

Through tangled sheets and missing mates,
They conquer fluff and dodgy fates.
With each twist, a laugh, a spin,
These fearless threads know they will win.

So when you wear that quirky gear,
Remember the shorts that faced their fear.
For in the chaos of cotton and wool,
It's the threads that stand, ever so cool.

Adorned in Bravery

In mismatched socks, we stride with pride,
Fear's a stretchy waistband, we won't hide.
With capes from grandma, and hats askew,
We dance through danger, for laughs ensue.

A rubber chicken tucked in our sleeve,
Tickling giants, we gleefully weave.
With jellybeans armed to take on the day,
We battle our fears in a goofy way.

Threads of the Resilient

In pajamas, armed with a spoon so grand,
We face all foes, like they were planned.
With spaghetti noodles, our lances we wield,
Courage is fueled by a pasta-filled shield.

We stitch our laughs in brave, silly tones,
And bake courage cookies filled with old bones.
With mischief in heart and a smile so wide,
We wrap ourselves up in joy as our guide.

Ships of the Strong

In paper boats, we sail the unknown,
With squirrels as captains, the seeds they've sown.
Through waters of laughter, we bravely float,
With marshmallow cannons, on whimsy we gloat.

Fears take a dive with each silly oar,
As we conquer seas with a knock-knock score.
With treasure maps drawn in crayon delight,
We navigate giggles till the stars shine bright.

The Weave of the Brave

With yarn and laughter, we knit up some cheer,
A sweater of courage that fits every fear.
Each stitch a giggle, each purl a pun,
Raveling doubts until they are none.

In hats like monsters, we strut down the lane,
With capes made of cheese, who could feel pain?
With laughter as glue, we brave every shame,
For we are the champions of silliness' game.

The Shielded Waist

In a world where pants may sag,
A waistguard stops the shameful brag.
With every step, I feel so bold,
My secrets safe, my guts are gold.

I once wore swag that fell to knees,
But now I flaunt with playful ease.
A shield of laughter, hugs all day,
My style's a riot, come what may.

Weaving the Fearless Spirit

With threads that stick like jelly beans,
I crafted courage from silly scenes.
Each stitch a giggle, every loop a cheer,
I'm the comical hero, never fear!

My fabric's made of bloopers past,
Where bravery's found in laughter cast.
When danger knocks, I bust a rhyme,
And flip my fears, I'm feeling fine!

Band of the Dauntless

Join my crew of jesters bold,
With bravery wrapped in jokes of old.
We march with giggles, stomps, and grins,
Taking on the world, let the fun begin!

A game of tag with shadows near,
But we just laugh, there's nothing to fear.
With every slip and every trip,
We dance through life, let courage rip!

The Unyielding Lattice

A tangled web of my own making,
With comedy, I dare to be shaking.
In this confusing, knotty maze,
I find my way through giggling haze.

I shout at fears, they run away,
My lattice strong on silly play.
With every twist and every turn,
I laugh at flames, I proudly burn!

Woven Dreams of the Fearless

In the closet a hero's costume waits,
With capes and tights for daring fates.
But when it's time to face the day,
Those jammies seem to win the fray.

Brave knights in shining cardboard gear,
With pizza slices, they conquer fear.
In the realm of sofa knights' delight,
The dragons run off at the pizza bite.

Fabric Between Heroes

Two friends stitching laughs across the seams,
Sewing patches on their wildest dreams.
With threads of jokes and stitches of fun,
They battle gloom until it's done.

A fabric torn with tales so bright,
In pajama pants, they take to flight.
Their laughter weaves a cozy spell,
As they trip and tumble, oh so swell.

Shields of the Unbroken

With pots for helmets and spoons afire,
They serve up courage, their true desire.
In kitchen battles, they raise a cheer,
While dodging flying mashed potatoes near.

Heroes in slippers, they take their stand,
Defending the fridge was always the plan.
With every snack, their strength does grow,
Banana peels? They dodge, but oh no!

Swathed in Determination

In blankets thick, they huddle tight,
As movie marathons replace the night.
With popcorn shields and candy canes,
They laugh at challenges, dismissing pains.

When morning comes, they stretch and yawn,
The quest involves a second dawn.
For conquering chores requires some flair,
While dancing 'round with unkempt hair.

Radiant Resolve

With my pants hitched up so high,
I march on through the pie in the sky.
Confidence waves like a silly flag,
As I juggle pies with a comedic wag.

No fear of slipping, no fear of slips,
Just laughter on my jokester's trips.
With every bounce, I twirl and spin,
A warrior's heart with a playful grin.

Grasping Grit

I wear my courage like a silly hat,
It flops and flutters, imagine that!
With every step, I wobble and sway,
As I duel with shadows and misfit prey.

I strike a pose, a battle dance,
In rubber boots, I take a chance.
With splats and plops, I unleash my might,
Who knew being brave could be such a sight?

Warriors in the Wind

As breezes swirl my hair around,
I march like royalty, oh, how profound!
But watch out for that gust, so dreary,
It spins me 'round and leaves me weary.

Laughing like a duck in a stormy fray,
I navigate life in a rollicking way.
With each gust, I sway and weave,
Oh, the tales of courage I believe!

Threads of Steel

I stitched my armor with glitter and zest,
In playful patterns, I feel like the best.
Wearing sequins that shimmer and shine,
A warrior's heart wrapped in designs so fine.

When the dragons come, I prance and twirl,
With threads of steel, I give them a whirl.
Their roars can't touch my festive flair,
As I conquer the day, without a care!

Molding Might

In pants too tight, I feel so bright,
A warrior's stance, in spandex delight.
With every stretch, I aim for the pie,
Fighting for snacks, oh my, oh my!

With socks that clash and shirt askew,
I'm here to conquer, who needs a crew?
My cape is a towel, my shield—a plate,
Bravado on high, I'm ready to plate!

Strength without Bounds

I lift my spoon, a mighty feat,
Ice cream awaits, oh sweet retreat.
My muscles flex with each brave scoop,
Defying gravity, I'm in the loop.

With burgers stacked, I'm set to go,
My appetite roars, a mighty show.
Like a knight of yore, in lunchtime battles,
Conquering fries and chicken rattles!

The Ties That Bind

In mismatched socks, I take my stand,
My fashion's bold, it's quite unplanned.
With laces tied in a wild dance,
I strut my stuff, oh what a chance!

Each belt I wear's a daring fight,
Holding me in with all its might.
Wobbling here, and zigzagging there,
Laughing at life, without a care!

Threads Against the Wind

The wind it howls, my hat takes flight,
Like a bird it sails, oh what a sight!
My cape is a scarf, whipping around,
In this fashion twist, I'm glory-bound!

With danger close, I face the jest,
A gust of laughter, I'm truly blessed.
I'll brave storms fierce, and clouds of gray,
With humor in hand, I'm here to play!

A Warrior's Heart

With a heart so bold, he braves the feat,
Chasing dragons down the street.
In his pajamas, sword in hand,
He fights off threats like it's all planned.

His armor's made of old tin cans,
He dances like no one understands.
With every clash, a silly shout,
Who knew courage had this clout?

Fabric of Bravery

In a cloak that's plaid, he struts about,
Claiming every laugh, with a funny pout.
Sprinkling glitter like it's a spell,
Making foes giggle, oh what a tell!

His cape is stitched from grandma's cloth,
While prancing like he's gone all froth.
With every step, the buttons pop,
'These threads of courage, never stop!'

Woven Resolve

Socks on hands, he takes a stance,
Chasing villains with a silly dance.
Each thread a laugh, each knot a cheer,
Who knew warriors had such flair?

With a helmet made of cereal, so bright,
He guards the realm from morning light.
In a world where humor reigns supreme,
He savors laughter like ice cream!

The Armor Within

Wrapped in bubble wrap, he feels so tough,
Bouncing off walls, 'Oh, this is enough!'
His shield? A trash can lid, oh so fine,
Defending all snacks, that's the design.

Each battle's won with a pun and cheer,
For conquering fears brings grins, oh dear!
A hero's heart beats loud with fun,
In this goofy life, we're all number one!

Straps of Strength

In the land of saggy pants,
We tightened up our fearless stance.
With laughter and a wiggle dance,
We chased our fears with comic prance.

A buddy slipped on a banana peel,
His courage made it all surreal.
He laughed so hard, it was the deal,
Heroes stumble, that's the real feel.

With jump ropes and silly songs,
We paired up to right the wrongs.
A tug of war is where it belongs,
And in the end, we all grew strong.

So if you think that fear will reign,
Just laugh it off, it's all in vain.
With stretchy straps, we'll entertain,
And wear our laughter like a chain.

Stitching the Spirit

In a sewing room with threads of cheer,
We patched our pride and faced the fear.
With needles and some jokes to share,
Each stitch a smile, beyond compare.

The fabric of our dreams was bright,
We stitched our hopes with all our might.
A bobbin dance in soft moonlight,
Turning frowns into sheer delight.

With every twirl and every weave,
We found the strength we all believe.
A quilt of giggles, let's achieve,
In stitches made, we will not cleave.

So gather 'round, let's sew today,
In colors bold, we'll find the way.
A seam of laughter on display,
'Tis our spirit that will sway!

Unyielding Resolve

With wobbly knees and glittered hats,
We gathered courage like happy cats.
Our resolve was firm, despite the spats,
No need for swords, we've got our bats.

In the face of pranks and funny tricks,
We grounded fears with tiny kicks.
With comic books and playful flicks,
We faced the world with goofy licks.

The bravest hearts were clownish souls,
We juggled fears like bowling bowls.
In zany acts, we'd reach our goals,
Nothing can stop our happy tolls.

So if you see your doubts appear,
Just wear a smile and have no fear.
With laughter loud and voices clear,
We found resolve, that's why we're here!

Bound by Fire

With flames of joy and playful sparks,
We lit our fears like glowing larks.
With crackling jokes and silly remarks,
We forged a path in the park's dark arcs.

Through blazing trails of silly pranks,
We danced around in laughter's banks.
With fireflies joining our shenanigans,
Our hearts were bright, like a thousand flanks.

No scorched earth, just fiery cheer,
We rallied all our friends so near.
With soft marshmallows and mugs of beer,
We burned our doubts without a fear.

So if you feel the chill of night,
Just gather round and hold on tight.
With flames of joy, we'll chase the fright,
In laughter's warmth, we find our light.

Armor of the Heart

My chest is strong, though soft within,
I wear my armor with a grin.
Made of giggles, laughs, and cheer,
It helps me face what I might fear.

When dragons roar and shadows fall,
I bounce around like a happy ball.
With silly moves and dance so spry,
I tackle trouble, oh my, oh my!

In battles of awkwardness, I thrive,
With my heart's armor, I come alive.
Oh, how I dodge the glares and stares,
Laughing my way past all the glares!

So if you see me prance about,
Know my rhymes are what I tout.
With jests and jigs, I've got a chart,
This is my lovely armor of heart!

Tapestry of Bravery

Woven threads of fun and jest,
In this tapestry, I do my best.
Each stitch a laugh, a wink, a grin,
Together we weave thick and thin.

Frogs on pogo sticks hop by,
Squirrels wear glasses, oh me, oh my!
Bravery comes with a splash and a dance,
In this silly world, we all take a chance.

With colors bright, like candy and cake,
This tapestry sways with every shake.
When fears loom large, I adjust my hat,
And laugh away worries—how about that?

So gather 'round and hear the tale,
Of a woven force that will never fail.
With humor blaring like a fanfare,
My tapestry of bravery we proudly wear!

Straps of Fortitude

I've got my straps, oh what a sight,
They keep me upright, day and night.
Each strap is silly, tied in a knot,
A wondrous fashion, believe it or not.

When hiccups come to steal my cheer,
I stretch my straps and persevere.
With every tug, I bounce and jig,
Jumping high like a wiggly pig!

If I trip, don't you fret,
My straps of fortitude never let.
One yank, one pull, I'm back on track,
With a chuckle and an awkward quack.

So if you see me slide or fall,
Remember my straps can conquer it all.
With a twist and a twirl, I stand in my boots,
Straps of fortitude, the silliest roots!

The Gritty Garment

In a gritty garment made of fluff,
I conquer the world with just enough.
It's not too tight and not too loose,
A cuddly shield that's of no excuse.

With pockets of giggles sewn on the side,
I tuck away fears that try to hide.
When trouble knocks, I strut with flair,
In my wacky threads, I'm free as air!

I twirl and bounce without a care,
My gritty garment, oh it's quite rare.
With every mishap, I'll laugh and smile,
Embracing each moment, one silly mile.

So join the fun, wear what you please,
In a gritty garment, laugh if you sneeze.
Together we rise, we dance, we play,
Embodying courage in our own funny way!

Resilience in Every Stitch

In the closet hangs a cape,
Sewn together with a tape.
Each thread a laugh, a jolly cheer,
Facing life without a fear.

Buttons fly with every dance,
Stitches pull in a wacky prance.
Loop and twist, the fabric's tight,
Worn with joy, it feels just right.

Though it frays, it holds its ground,
Bouncing back, it spins around.
A patch here, a patch there,
Feeling bold beyond compare.

With a wink and a silly grin,
Every barrier's just a spin.
In this quilt of quirks and zest,
We wear our laughter; we are blessed.

The Fabric of Fearlessness

A shirt made from a rainbow's light,
Dares to laugh at every fright.
Each color stitched with giggles bright,
Facing monsters in the night.

Pockets deep for all my dreams,
Filling them with silly schemes.
A cape that jumps with every hop,
In this fabric, fears just stop.

Hems that tickle, seams that tease,
Worn with pride and lots of ease.
Swirling laughter in every fold,
This wear is worth its weight in gold.

With a sassy shake and shimmy flair,
It sways in rhythm, without a care.
Bold and bright, we'll make the scene,
In this garb, we're almost mean!

Threads of Tenacity

A sock with stripes and polka dots,
Holds the courage in its knots.
With every stumble, every fall,
It giggles up and stands up tall.

Silly hats with feathers bright,
Dancing merrily in the night.
Quirky ties that twist and spin,
Show the fun that's deep within.

Denim dreams with pockets wide,
They catch the fears that tried to hide.
A belt with squeaks that make you grin,
Adventures start where bold begins.

So put that shirt and pants on right,
With every laugh, face down the fright.
In this outfit, joy's a must,
Life's a game; let's play, we trust!

The Cloak of the Dauntless

A cloak adorned with buttons bright,
Makes the shadows dance with light.
Swishing through with every glide,
Bravely worn, there's naught to hide.

It billows out, a tidal wave,
Carrying all the brave and brave.
With pockets full of silly tricks,
We're off to tackle life's high kicks.

Every flap a playful cheer,
Worn by those who laugh at fear.
In this cloak, no burden stays,
Comedic joy in every phase.

So twirl around, let laughter ring,
With every spin, you'll feel like a king.
Adventurers in each funny fold,
In this garment, be brave and bold!

Gritted Teeth and Woven Threads

With grit in our smiles, we tackle the day,
Threads woven tight, come what may.
The world throws its jests, we laugh them away,
In the fabric of life, we choose our ballet.

Worn shoes squeak a tune, they dance on the street,
We strut like peacocks, embracing defeat.
With each little stumble, we rise to our feet,
These woven connections make our lives sweet.

A patchwork of stories, each thread tells a tale,
With mismatched intentions, we laugh without fail.
The colors may clash, but that's how we sail,
Through storms and through sunshine, we will prevail.

So here's to the fabric that holds us so tight,
In the dance of our lives, we twirl with delight.
With gritted teeth and threads glowing bright,
We weave our own magic, oh what a sight!

Points of Pride

With points of pride, we strut around,
In socks with holes that squeak as they sound.
We collect our quirks, a treasure profound,
In the carnival of life, we dance unbound.

Our hats are too big, our pants are too small,
Yet we wear them with flair, standing proud and tall.
In a world full of norms, we're having a ball,
Gathering giggles, we'll conquer it all.

Each wacky mishap, a badge on our chest,
In costumes of chaos, we feel truly blessed.
With laughter as armor, we face every test,
In a patchwork of joy, we continue our fest.

So cheers to the odd, the quirky and bright,
In the garden of laughter, everything's right.
With points of pride shining, we reach for the light,
Creating a tapestry, bold and outright!

Edges of Energy

On the edges of energy, we laugh and we leap,
In zany adventures, where no one can sleep.
With coffee on hand and no time to keep,
A merry band of jesters, in joy we steep.

Our giggles take flight like balloons in the air,
In absurd little moments, we shed all despair.
From tripping on shoelaces to dancing a square,
We gather the whimsy, a curious flair.

In the circus of life, we juggle our woes,
With each slip and stumble, our laughter just flows.
With whimsical hearts, our joy truly grows,
We chase silly dreams wherever it goes.

So onward we charge, with sparkles and cheer,
On the edges of madness, we hold our hearts dear.
In the dance of our lives, let's bring on the jeer,
For laughter's our armor, it conquers all fear!

Textiles of Triumph

In textiles of triumph, we stitch up the fun,
Our needles are laughter, we've only just begun.
With patches of joy, we've already won,
In this crazy quilt life, we're second to none.

With threads of mishaps that weave us so tight,
We gather our moments, all quirky and bright.
From kitchen disasters to magical flights,
We'll quilt our own fortunes, by day and by night.

So bring on the chaos, let's blend all the hues,
With clumsy connections, we'll never lose.
In the fabric of friendship, each laugh is a fuse,
Creating a masterpiece, with nothing to snooze.

So here's to the threads that connect us with glee,
In this tapestry woven with warmth, can't you see?
With textiles of triumph, forever we'll be,
Dancing through life, in joyful esprit!

Chain of the Unfaltering.

In a world where fear takes a seat,
A chain of laughter helps us compete.
With silly hats and wobbly shoes,
We strut with pride, not singing the blues.

We stumble and trip, yet light on our toes,
In the face of a scare, we strike a pose.
With rubber chickens and tickler sticks,
We conquer our fears with all our quirks.

Our chain won't break, it's linked with delight,
Each giggle we share ignites a bright light.
Not a sword, not a shield, it's laughter each day,
A bonding of hearts in the silliest way.

Let's dance in the rain and jump in the mud,
With courage that comes not from a thud.
For in this wild chain, we bravely unite,
With joy as our armor, we soar into night.

Courage's Embrace

In pajamas adorned, we face our fears,
With capes made of blankets and leaping cheers.
A fortress of giggles wraps us so tight,
As monsters retreat at the squeak of our fight.

With cookies in hand, we march to our fate,
Each crunching sound makes the shadows abate.
We don the brave pants, right over our jams,
Creating a kingdom of fun-loving hams.

In board games of bravery, we boldly play,
Laughing at dangers that stand in our way.
With every wild roll of the dice we embrace,
A leap into laughter, a comical race.

With pets as our steeds and laughter as guide,
We charge into chaos, no need to hide.
In this raucous parade, let worries disperse,
With courage that flourishes, the humor is terse.

Shadows and Shields

Shadows may lurk, but we've got a plan,
With peanut butter swords, we're a daring band.
With giggles as shields, and laughter our might,
We tackle the goblins that give us a fright.

In the midst of the haze, we wear goofy grins,
With marshmallow armor, our fun never thins.
As shadows creep closer, we strike with our charm,
Wielding colorful pillows to bring down the harm.

Each squeaky response sets the tension at bay,
With a hop and a skip, we scare fears away.
In this comical quest, we rise up as one,
Against the dark shadows, we shine like the sun.

So, grab your plush shields; let's forge ahead,
With ticklish attacks, we'll plow through instead.
In the realm of the brave, our laughter reveals,
A friendship that's forged with unbreakable feels.

Threads of Valor.

With threads of bright colors, we stitch up our fears,
Crafting capes of giggles and hats made of cheers.
In a workshop of whimsy, we fashion our fate,
Each stitch tells a story, and laughter won't wait.

As we weave tales of courage with threads bold and bright,
Our humor ignites like a spark in the night.
With twirls and with swirls, we dance through the day,
Embroidered in joy, tossing worries away.

In the fabric of friendship, we find what we seek,
A patchwork of laughter in every small peek.
For courage is found in the stitches and seams,
Where together we build our most whimsical dreams.

So, let's thread up our worries, we'll fashion delight,
With every funny twist, we're taking to flight.
In a world full of fabric and tales yet untold,
We'll craft our adventures with stitches of gold.

Sinews of Resolve

In a world where fears take flight,
A chicken danced under the moonlight.
With a brave little heart, it flapped about,
Claiming all dragons would soon face doubt.

Through puddles it pranced, mud on its beak,
Swearing that bravery made it unique.
Each cluck a rally, each wiggle a cheer,
Who knew combat was hiding in sheer?

But then came the wolf, fur shiny and sly,
The chicken then thought, 'Should I really try?'
With auto-determined joy, it took a stand,
Yelling out threats with a winged hand.

So remember this tale when feeling low,
Even cloaked in feathers, great courage can grow.
With laughter and clucks, don't ever back down,
Even a fowl can wear valor's crown.

Mantle of the Brave

A snail set off with dreams too grand,
Wore a cape made of cheese, how cool was that brand!
It dazzled the mice, while frogs gave a cheer,
'You'll outrun the world, we've nothing to fear!'

But then came a puddle, immense as the sea,
The snail thought, 'Could this be the end of me?'
With a wiggle and wobble, it slid right through,
Leaving behind all its friends feeling blue.

Yet a turtle shouted, 'Just don't paint it red!'
Snails and turtles? A plan in their head.
They'd lasso the moon with a thread of delight,
Proving true courage can emerge each night.

So if your cheese cape gets stuck in a crack,
Remember that laughter can put you back on track.
When you walk with the brave, it gets quite absurd,
Even slowpokes can dance if you humor a bird!

Wyvern's Hold

A cat with a sword, what an odd sight,
Claimed itself royal, by moon's silver light.
With a tail that could swish any foe right away,
It fought shadows nightly in a grand display.

But then came the dragon, a foe sharp of claw,
The cat raised its sword with a confident paw.
But alas, it slipped on a sweet, gooey treat,
Flew through the air, landing hard on its feet.

The dragon just giggled, bright breath in the sky,
'Thought you were fierce, don't make me laugh cry!'
The swaggering cat regained lofty ground,
With purrs and bravado, they twirled all around.

In the end, they shared tales of valor and cheer,
In a world full of jest, there's nothing to fear.
So wield your play sword, dance 'till you sweat,
For every brave heart's a hilarious bet!

The Tenacious Bind

Two socks set sail on an ocean of grime,
Seeking glory with every crook in their mime.
'Think of the socks we'll save from the heap!'
They vowed, voice entwined, 'This mission's for keeps!'

They traveled through dust bunnies, dodged Barbie's shoes,
Chasing elusive lint that would make them choose.
With laughter a-plenty, they slipped and they slid,
Socks with a purpose, who knew they were hid?

At last they found freedom from chasms so deep,
Promised to tread where no other would creep.
A sock revolution, that sounds quite absurd,
So throw on your best, the world's getting stirred!

For whenever you're stuck, just dance through the fray,
Even misfits can find the right fun in the fray.
With socks on their feet, a true tale they'll spin,
A journey of laughter that'll always begin.

Threads of Tenacity

In a world so wobbly, watch me twirl,
With stitches of bravery, I give it a whirl.
I trip on my cape, oh what a show!
But watch out, I'm dancing, despite the slow flow.

With threads that hold stories of laughter and cheer,
I wear them like armor, no sign of fear.
Each knot is a giggle, each seam is a grin,
Oh, the fun in the folly, where do I begin?

I strut like a peacock, with fabric so bright,
Flaunting my courage, I take to the night.
And when I fall over, in style I land,
With a wink and a laugh, it's all so well planned.

So if life gets tricky, just give it a spin,
With threads of tenacity, you're sure to win.
Laugh at the tumbles, they're part of the game,
With fabric of fun, we'll never be the same!

Sash of the Fearless

A sash tied on tight, let's make it a race,
I'll sprint through the garden, give laughter a place.
With each little stumble, I wiggle and shake,
Fearless, I trip on my own little wake.

This fabric's my buddy, my friend in despair,
When I wear it too high, it gets caught in my hair.
But off with a giggle, I jiggle and sway,
In a dance quite ridiculous, I'll show you the way.

I wrap it around me, oh what a delight,
I twirl and I whirl, like a kite in flight.
If life's just a circus, I'm leading the show,
With a sash that shows bravado, come join the flow!

So strut with your sash, let the world see you shine,
With laughter and courage, we'll toast with some wine.
For the wild and the free, let your spirit be fierce,
In this game of silliness, let joy be our pierce!

Emblem of Strength

With an emblem so bold, I declare my might,
But wait, is that mud? What a comical sight!
I'm a warrior wobbly, I'll fight to the end,
With dignity trembling, I'm still on the mend.

My emblem's a badge of the times that I've tripped,
Through puddles and pranks, I've poorly equipped.
With strength in my laughter, I tackle it all,
In this jolly arena, I'm bound to have a ball.

Each bruise tells a story, both funny and bright,
In this armor of jest, I'm ready to fight.
Though my sword is a spoon and my shield's made of cheese,
Let's charge into silliness, if you please!

So cheer for the emblem that proudly displays,
The strength in the giggles, the joy of the play.
For in every stammer and slip that we make,
There's power in laughter; it's yours for the take!

Ribbon of Resoluteness

With a ribbon so loose, I can't quite take flight,
I trip on my mission, but oh, what a sight!
Resolute in my goals, though wobbly and spry,
I dance through the chaos, like clouds in the sky.

Each loop tells a tale of my clumsy delight,
Like a cat in a tree, I'll be fine — or I might!
But hey, with determination, I climb and I laugh,
In this ribbon of fun, I'm my own autograph.

Tangled and teetering, I'm still going strong,
For the path might be bumpy, but I'm in for the throng.
With a flip and a flourish, I'll joust with the breeze,
This ribbon's my spirit, it dances with ease.

So flash that bright ribbon, let your heart steer,
Through the giggles and tumbles, we'll conquer the fear.
For in laughter, we find the true essence of zest,
In this parade of the silly, we're all truly blessed!

The Colors of Courage

In a world bright and bold,
Heroes wear hues of gold.
With capes that flap and twirl,
They tumble, oh what a whirl!

One brave knight in red's delight,
Trips on shoes that aren't quite right.
He laughs it off with a wink,
Says, "Courage comes from the brink!"

Blue tights so tight, a tad absurd,
With a cape that flies like a bird.
But hey, who needs style or grace,
When you can run at a silly pace!

So paint your fears in every shade,
In funny hues, let jokes invade.
For courage isn't how you stand,
But how you trip with a laugh unplanned!

Woven Whispers of Will

Once a hero, brave and spry,
Tried to conquer the chicken pie.
With courage sewn in every seam,
His appetite held a crazy dream!

He took a fork and gave a poke,
Declared it strong, despite the yolk.
His friends all laughed, they called him bold,
As he wrestled with crust that wouldn't fold!

A giant bite, oh what a sight,
Chicken fled, in a chaotic flight!
With every chew, a giggle slips,
For courage comes in messy trips.

So arm yourself with forks and pies,
And wear your courage in funny ties.
For in this feast where jokes abound,
True strength is everywhere 'round!

The Song of the Spirited

Oh sing the song of brave delight,
Where courage dances through the night.
With a goofy jig and a wobbly spin,
Who knew that bold could start with a grin?

A sassy bard, with lute in tow,
Sings tales of mishaps, steals the show.
With every strum, a giggle grows,
For courage blooms in funny throes!

The trolls in the tale just want some fun,
Tripping over their two left feet, they run.
Each stumble earns a hearty cheer,
For laughter's the bravest thing, oh dear!

So raise a glass to gutsy souls,
Who laugh and dance and make us whole.
For in this jolly, spirited throng,
Courage is found in every song!

A Tapestry of Conquest

In the marketplace of doubts and fears,
Fighters barter with silly sneers.
One trades tales of dragon fright,
While another laughs at a rainbow kite!

A tapestry spun of daring lore,
With threads of laughter from every floor.
Each hero's stitch, a quirk to behold,
In a colorful weave that defies the cold!

When armor clinks, it's more than tough,
It's filled with funny, and that's enough!
For in this craft of bold delight,
True valiance shines in jest so bright.

So thread your needle with hopes and dreams,
Stitch in the giggles, let laughter beam.
For conquest awaits in each silly crack,
And courage wears the best of a laugh-back!

The Courageous Fabric

In a world of cotton and thread,
Fabrics whisper secrets unsaid.
One sock claims it's bold and brave,
While the other just wants to wave!

The shirts strut and boast with pride,
While the pants just hope to hide.
But lo! A stain, a drip, a thrill,
Turns fashion's moments into a chill!

With every stitch, laughter does grow,
As we sew our tales from high to low.
Even patches have stories to tell,
Of washing machine battles, oh so swell!

So gather your garments, don't be shy,
Let whimsical threads lift your spirits high!
In this playful fabric, courage is spun,
Dressing in joy is how we have fun!

A Tapestry of Grit

Behold the tapestry, a quirky sight,
With llamas dancing in the moonlight.
Each thread tells tales, some awkward and bold,
Of adventures misfit, but happily told!

There's a patch where socks go to speak,
Whispering secrets, both silly and weak.
A courageous collar that won't sit still,
Dreams of capes when you walk up that hill!

The buttons giggle, the zippers clink,
A knot of laughter, don't you think?
With every weave, a chuckle or two,
Creating a fabric both funny and true!

So let's wear this tapestry with flair,
A bold design, beyond compare.
For laughter and grit are sewn by the yard,
In a world of fun, we'll always play hard!

Courage in Every Thread

Today's the day, let's give it a twirl,
In a wild outfit, let confidence swirl.
A plaid that squeaks and a polka dot cheer,
We'll strut down the street without a hint of fear!

Stitches of bravery in every seam,
Transforming life into a fabric dream.
Fluffy and fun, like a giant marshmallow,
With every outfit, we'll grab the gallow!

Labels with stories and patches of flair,
Some have superpowers, others just air.
But where bravery meets a silly design,
Laughter erupts, it's simply divine!

So shake off the doubt, and embrace your thread,
In a world of fashion, let joy be spread.
For the bolder the colors, the braver we feel,
With laughter entwined, it's surely a deal!

The Emblem of Tenacity

There once was a patch with a heart so bright,
It wore mismatched socks, ready for fright.
Each evening it promised to fight its fray,
While winking at socks that went out to play!

With buttons that dance and ribbons that sing,
This emblem of joy wears a crown made of bling.
It laughed at the stains that tried to cause fuss,
In the face of a spill, it just made a fuss!

Threads woven tightly with gags and some puns,
This banner of giggles has captured our fun.
Unraveling worries like yarn from a spool,
This emblem of grit keeps us all cool!

So don on your patterns and wear them with glee,
For the more that we share, the lighter we'll be.
In the tapestry of life, be the thread that is bright,
A stitch of pure laughter, a dazzling sight!

The Courageous Weave

In the loom of life, we take a thread,
Woven with laughter, not filled with dread.
A stitch of silliness, bold and bright,
Tied with a knot that feels just right.

With fabric of humor, we'll dance in glee,
A tapestry of courage for you and me.
We wear our quirks like a dazzling cloak,
Each laugh a thread in this joyful joke.

So grab your yarn and knit away,
Fortitude woven in a funny way.
When fears arise, we'll just chuckle and grin,
For with humor's touch, we always win.

Embrace your colors, let your spirit fly,
We're all a patchwork in the big sky.
In this whimsical weave, let's strut and sway,
For courage is laughter - come join the play!

A Guardian's Girdle

They say a guardian wears a strong belt,
But mine's made of giggles, and oh, how it felt!
With a waistband of jokes and pockets of cheer,
My bravery's fashion, oh-so-dear!

When danger calls, I just do a dance,
In my silly get-up, I take a chance.
With a twirl of my hips, the shadows all flee,
That girdle of joy, it's magic, you see!

My buckle's a cupcake, it's sweet and it's grand,
With frosting of courage, it's perfectly planned.
I strut like a peacock, fluffs in the air,
For in this outfit, I have not a care.

So let laughter be armor, and smiles be my shield,
In this goofy ensemble, I never will yield.
For in the arena of life, come what may,
With humor as my girdle, I'm ready to play!

Bound for Greatness

Bounding forth, with a skip and a hop,
My trusty cloak of giggles never will stop.
With a cape made of puns and a hat of delight,
I'll conquer my fears with a joke in the night.

In the realm of the brave, where terrors reside,
I dance bravely forth, with myself as my guide.
With banter and quips, I'll lighten the air,
Each chuckle a beacon, I'm stripped of all fear.

I'm tangled in laughter, wrapped up so tight,
My heart full of grit, and my pants oh-so-bright.
With a skip and a sneeze, I'll turn frowns to beams,
For greatness is silly, or so it seems.

So let's march together, oh what a parade!
In this jovial journey, no need to be afraid.
For laughter is courage, a light as it pings,
And bound for the great, oh, the joy that it brings!

The Tapestry of Fearlessness

Woven with echoes of laughter and cheer,
A tapestry bright, dispelling our fear.
With threads of bright colors, so wild and so free,
We stitch up our courage for all to see!

In the fabric of friendship, we sew and we play,
With tickles and giggles, we brighten the day.
Our needles are giggles, our scissors, pure fun,
In this crafty adventure, we've already won!

Each patch is a story, a jest and a jest,
In this quilt of bravery, we're all at our best.
When troubles arise, we'll just pull a thread,
And weave in a punchline instead of dread.

So let's knot our humor and fringe out our fears,
In this whirling embrace, we'll conquer with cheers.
For in the large canvas of life's crazy spree,
Our tapestry gleams with sweet harmony!

Barefoot in Bravery

When the ground feels hot as toast,
I kick my shoes with utmost boast.
With every step, I feel so free,
Who needs shoes, just look at me!

My friends all laugh, they think I'm mad,
Yet barefoot life makes me feel glad.
In every puddle, splashes fly,
It's fun to jump and watch them cry!

A brave parade with toes aglow,
No socks to hold me back, oh no!
I dance on grass and poke the ants,
In every misstep, I take my chance!

So here I stand, with sunny glee,
Who knew my feet could really soar?
I'll strut my daring, house of cheer,
All in the joy, of lacking fear!

Kinship of the Bold

A band of friends, we take on leaps,
With laughter loud, as courage creeps.
No challenge great can bring us down,
    We wear our guts like a crown!

We tell tall tales and boast of might,
    Fighting shadows in the night.
A monster lurks behind the tree,
Tag, you're it — it's just silly me!

In costumes bright, we strut about,
With capes and dreams, we scream and shout.
A warrior squad, so brave and bright,
    Each goofy grin a pure delight!

Our kinship strong, but clumsy too,
As we tumble, fall, and start anew.
Together we dance, a joyful fest,
In a world where fun is truly blessed!

Adorned in Valor

With cardboard shields and tin foil crowns,
We march around in our silly gowns.
We're knights of yore in this garden war,
Defending realms behind the door!

We wield our sticks like mighty swords,
As we pretend to fight with words.
The dragon's fierce is just a cat,
But who needs skill when you've got that?

With paper capes, we swirl with grace,
Pretending we can conquer space.
Our eyes ablaze with hero dreams,
In the cosmos, laughter gleams!

So raise a cheer for our great squad,
The fearless fools that might look odd.
In every quest, we boldly play,
Our valor shines in a goofy way!

The Huers of Hope

With nets of dreams, we catch the stars,
And plan our trips to Mars and bars.
We laugh and scheme, our laughter loud,
Here come the brave, let's make 'em proud!

We doodle maps on napkins bright,
As we plot out our daring flight.
With hopes so high, we take our stance,
Who needs a plan? Let's risk a chance!

We sell our dreams like lemonade,
With each sip taken, laughter made.
Our lemonade stands are pure delight,
Full of hope, we shine so bright!

So pack your snacks and wear a grin,
Join the huers, let fun begin!
Together we'll chase the faintest light,
In a world where dreams take flight!

The Weaving of Hope

In a loom of dreams, we twist and turn,
Yarns of laughter, a lesson to learn.
Threads of boldness, mixed with some glee,
Stitching our quirks in a tapestry.

Fabrics of fortune, they wrinkle and play,
Colors of courage brighten the day.
With each little knot, a giggle is sown,
Crafting our joy in a world of our own.

The patterns we make, a comical show,
Fuzzy and bright, like a clown's peachy glow.
We dance with the fibers of whimsy and cheer,
Creating the fabric of what we hold dear.

So let us all weave with laughter and fun,
A blanket of friendship, we're never outdone.
With threads of hope spun around every seam,
We bask in the joy of our dazzling dream.

The Edges of Essentiality

In a world of essentials, we often forget,
To laugh at the quirks that cause us to fret.
For in every corner, a jest we will find,
In the edges of life, it's humor that binds.

A spoon on the floor makes a raucous sound,
While slipping on socks can leave us quite bound.
The secret to living, is not just to cope,
But to savor each blunder with a sprinkle of hope.

The essentials are many, but laughter's a gem,
A potion for courage, it's fun to condemn.
When life hands you hiccups, just chuckle and smile,
For jest is the fuel that will take you a mile.

So gather your giggles and wear them with pride,
In the edges of life, let your spirit abide.
With joy as our shield, and a wink from above,
We'll dance through each challenge, hand in glove.

Ties that Conquer

Ties that we wear, oh what a sight,
From polka dots, stripes, to colors so bright.
With each little knot, a chuckle will rise,
As they slip and they slide, what a comical surprise!

A cape made of plaid, a joy for the view,
When they trip on their laces, they've made quite the crew.
In a world full of ties, let's playfully twist,
Wearing laughter as armor, you cannot resist.

Get tangled in giggles, let's bind it with cheer,
For ties that we conquer, are made of good humor.
With each silly dance and whimsical spin,
Every loop is a victory—let the fun begin!

So knot up your worries and roll with the flow,
For in this grand journey, we're never alone.
Together we conquer, with ties of delight,
We'll laugh through the challenges, hearts so light.

Emblems of the Resolute

With badges of laughter pinned close to the heart,
We charge into life, oh, what a fine art!
Emblems of strength, with a wink and a grin,
In the silly skirmishes, we always win!

In capes made of dreams, we march forth in style,
Each step filled with giggles that stretch for a mile.
When ladders of laughter are climbed up so high,
Who knew goofiness could help us to fly?

Cracking up at the falls, with our comrades in tow,
We wear our resolve like a majestic show.
For every misstep brings a chorus of cheer,
And the laughter we've woven rings crystal clear.

So don your emblems, let your spirit ignite,
March into mischief, hearts bursting with light.
In the face of the silly, we scheme and we jest,
With smiles our companions, we're truly blessed!

Fabric of Unshakeable Faith

In a world where socks disappear,
I wear my courage without fear.
Though laundry monsters steal with glee,
My faith wraps snugly around me.

When doubts come sneaking 'round my head,
I tell them, 'No! I'm not misled!'
With every twist and every turn,
I chuckle, for there's much to learn.

With fabric soft and pattern bright,
I prance through day and dance at night.
Each patch a tale of battles won,
With laughter loud, my heart's undone.

So here's to threads of vibrant hue,
That lifts me up when skies aren't blue.
In every stitch, my joy's embrace,
I strut my stuff with style and grace.

The Stronghold Wrap

When worries knock upon my door,
I wrap myself, then I'll outscore.
A blanket of absurd delight,
Keeps silliness within my sight.

With every loop, I stitch a joke,
A fortress made of silly smoke.
The nightstand's filled with crazy dreams,
Where courage giggles and it beams.

So if you find my jokes too silly,
Just know my heart's never too frilly.
This armor's made for laughs, not fights,
I wrap myself in carefree nights.

Laughing with my trusty teddy,
In my stronghold, I feel quite ready.
To face the world with chuckles loud,
As I parade a joyful crowd.

Veil of the Valiant

With a veil that's light and pretend,
I'm here to make you laugh, my friend.
It shimmers like a disco ball,
And makes me feel ten feet tall.

When courage falters, I just giggle,
This cape can make the bravest wiggle.
A flouncy thing that floats and sways,
My daring self in silly ways.

With every toss and playful glance,
The bravest hearts can't help but dance.
My veil's disguise is pure delight,
Turning woes into a comedy fight.

So join the fun, let spirits soar,
In joy and laughter, we'll explore.
With a giggle, I'll take my flight,
Boldly shining in the night.

Cincture of Inner Fire

Around my waist, a vibrant band,
It sparks with silliness quite grand.
Though flames of courage make me bold,
I dance like I'm not getting old.

With a cincture made of jokes and jests,
I bear the world's wobbly tests.
When life gets tough, I twist and swear,
With every laugh, I cast despair.

It's wide enough to store my dreams,
And keep me warm with laughter's beams.
Each twist, a charmer of the night,
My spirit sings, my soul takes flight.

So here's my seal of funny fire,
That lifts me higher, never tires.
In laughter's embers, I shall live,
And dance with joy, that's what I give.

Straps of the Brave

On my waist, a ribbon tied,
Each venture's a thrilling ride!
With every step, I might just trip,
But watch me dance, and laugh, and flip!

I strut with swagger, bold and bright,
Wobbling left, then veering right.
In life's circus, I'm a clown,
Wearing my courage like a crown!

My friends all cheer, they shout and beam,
As I leap high, a silly dream.
Their giggles echo, loud and clear,
In this crazy game, I persevere!

So if you stumble, don't you pout,
Let joy and laughter swirl about.
With every knot, I tie my fate,
Embracing fun, I celebrate!

Pillars of Positivity

I built my home on joyful beams,
With laughter's echo, bursting seams.
Each quirk and twist, a funny feat,
In my wide palace, life's a treat!

From dawn till dusk, I smile so wide,
A hero's cape I wear with pride.
My friends come join, with giggles loud,
We dance and skip, a merry crowd!

When worries prod, I juggle hope,
Clumsily taking every slope.
With every flop, a fun surprise,
My pillars rise beneath the skies!

So if you find your mood feels grim,
Just join this wobbly, joyful whim.
Together we'll laugh, let's make a toast,
To all life's quirks, we'll love the most!

Weaving Fortitude

With threads of joy, I craft my fate,
Each stitch a giggle, never late.
In the tapestry of silly dreams,
Life's mishaps turn to laughter streams!

When the fabric frays, I just embrace,
With twirling moves, I find my grace.
Like a jester in grand attire,
I laugh and dance, lift spirits higher!

From wobbling lines to tangled knots,
Every misstep fills my plots.
I weave my tale with threads of cheer,
In this zany world, I persevere!

So grab your threads and join the fun,
Let's weave together, everyone!
With every laugh, we'll stitch and sew,
Our fortitude in joy will glow!

Strength Adorned

Adorned with laughs, I walk with flair,
A charm of courage, beyond compare.
With silly hats and shoes so bright,
My goofy style is pure delight!

Life's a parade, and I'm the star,
With dance moves wacky, yet bizarre.
I twirl and spin, I trip and fall,
But laughter's magic conquers all!

In this grand show, I'm never shy,
With every slip, I reach for the sky.
Grace is overrated, I'll declare,
While joy and giggles fill the air!

So come and join this merry spree,
Wear your quirks like jewelry!
With strength adorned in laughter sweet,
Together we'll make life's rhythm beat!

Cloak of the Indomitable

A cape made of laughter, it flows in the breeze,
Worn over pajamas, it aims to please.
With pockets of snacks that never run dry,
It makes even the grumpiest spirit fly.

When foes come to tease, I just strike a pose,
With a wink and a grin, I decompose.
"You think you can scare me? Not a chance, my friend!"
In this silly outfit, all worries suspend.

The seams are quite sturdy, stitched with a dream,
I'm ready for anything, or so it would seem.
A cape made of courage, I'll wear it with glee,
And dance through the doubt like it's just a cup of tea.

So here's to the fabric of brave, joyful hearts,
That lifts us through trials and quirky life parts.
For every odd moment, I'm proud to partake,
With my cloak on my shoulders, I'm never a fake.

Shield Worn with Pride

A shield made of pizza, it's greasy and round,
With slices of courage, my heroes abound.
Deflecting all issues with crusty finesse,
I stand in the kitchen and wear my success.

When bullies come knocking, I just take a bite,
With cheese as my armor, I'm ready to fight.
"What's that? You're mocking? Well, take a seat!"
I'll toss you a slice—now you can't be beat!

So bring on your snacks, your jabs, and your jests,
I'll shield myself proudly, ignoring your tests.
With garlic bread handles, this armor's legit,
My culinary pride never lets me quit.

So here's to my shield, with toppings galore,
It's never quite boring, it's a mouthful of lore.
For every encounter, I'll savor the taste,
Worn with pride, this shield lets me feast with no haste.

Badge of Defiance

A badge made of gum that sticks to my jeans,
It tells all the world I'm chasing my dreams.
With glittery sparkles that shimmer and shine,
I wear it with joy, proudly marking my line.

When people say, "Quit!" I just pop my gum,
With a loud, boisterous smack, I know how to stun.
"You want me to listen? Well, chew on this gum!"
It's a badge of defiance, I'm never a bum!

So here's to the rebel, the sparkly cheer,
With gum as my emblem, I have nothing to fear.
For when life gets sticky, I'll blow bubbles wide,
With a badge made of gum, I'll take life in stride.

Through all the ruckus, I'll stand proud and tall,
A badge of great laughter, I'll conquer it all.
With a twist and a twirl, I'll face what's ahead,
With gum on my side, I've nothing to dread.

Ties that Bind

With shoelaces tangled, I'm ready to go,
These links to my pals make my courage grow.
We skip through the chaos, as strong as a team,
Laughing at fumbles, living the dream.

A loop and a twist, we're a curious bunch,
A circus of quirks, ready for lunch!
When one of us tumbles, we giggle and cheer,
With ties that keep us, we've nothing to fear.

Through slippery sidewalks and puddles of fun,
We're strict with our orders, no one weighs a ton!
With our friendship so sturdy, not even a rift,
Could break up our laughter, it's our greatest gift.

So here's to the bonds that keep us aligned,
With giggles and snacks, our hearts intertwined.
Together we wander, unchained and unlined,
With ties that bind joy, let our laughter remind.

Warrior's Embrace

In the land of silly fights,
A warrior tripped over his tights.
With a wink and a grin,
He danced in the din!

He claimed it was style, not a slip,
As he did a triumphant flip.
With laughter so bright,
He turned wrongs to right!

With armor made out of cheese,
He rode off in a breeze.
His foes laughed so hard,
They forgot to stand guard!

In battle, he'd prance,
In his wobbly dance.
The legend went forth,
He charmed foes to mirth!

Fabric of Valor

A knight with a cape made of fur,
Claimed to be fierce, but then a purr!
He petted his steed,
And they both took heed—

To shine in the sun and not stir!
In fights, he would twirl and he'd whirl,
But mostly he'd chat
With the dog named Matt!

His armor was shiny and blue,
And the helm had a bright smile, too!
When trouble drew near,
He'd offer a cheer,

Saying, "Who's up for a stew?"
His foes, in a puzzled trance,
Joined him for lunch
And forgot how to punch!

Courage Woven in Threads

In a shirt that was stitched with a joke,
A daring young lad, oh what a bloke!
He challenged a troll,
With soft words so dull,

And offered him pie with a poke.
The troll, in a fit, let out a laugh,
And soon shared his bread,
While they danced instead!

With laughter like music that flows,
They forgot all their ancient old woes.
With courage so bright,
They danced through the night,

In the threads where humor now grows.

Girdle of Resolve

With a girdle so bright, made of strings,
He stepped into battle, and what a fling!
He tripped on his lace,
And fell on his face,

But laughed it off, claiming, "I'm king!"
His foes, caught off guard by this sight,
Joined him in the fun,
As they all came undone!

In armor adorned with a grin,
They danced as the fight wore thin.
With each silly flop,
The laughter won't stop—

In battles where camaraderie spins!

Fables Tied in Fiber

There once was a knight with pants so tight,
He laughed with a jig, what a silly sight!
His armor clanked loud, like a marching band,
As he twirled in the field, sword held in hand.

With courage wrapped round his wobbly waist,
He danced with the dragons, moving with haste.
He took a bold leap, felt a sudden snare,
And landed right in a green, furry chair!

The villagers chuckled, they said with glee,
"Look at the knight, as brave as can be!"
With a wink and a grin, he took it in stride,
Wearing laughter like armor, he wore it with pride.

Entwined in Audacity

In a castle so grand, with a jester so spry,
He wore a big cape, saying, 'Watch me fly!'
With a heart full of dreams, he leaped in the air,
And tripped on a cat, who knew he was there!

He spun like a top, a most fumbled ballet,
'Then I'll conquer my fears, I say, come what may!'
The crowd erupted with laughter and cheer,
As he rolled down the hill, with no hint of fear!

With ribbons and bows, all tangled with pride,
Our fool of a friend wore his courage outside.
Though he fell with a flop, he stood up so tall,
In the game of the brave, he conquered it all!

The Passionate Pattern

In a land where the socks had a colorful twist,
Lived a hero who dreamed to be on the list.
With polka dots shining and stripes swirled tight,
He laughed at the dragons with sheer delight.

He'd jump and he'd stomp, then he'd twirl on a dime,
In pajamas so bright, he felt quite sublime.
'Fear not!' he would call, 'for today is the day,
I'll dance with the trolls in my wacky array!'

The trolls were perplexed, they chuckled and snorted,
As the hero pranced on, quite brightly supported.
Through giggles and glee, they forgot all their fights,
As he spun in his jammies, oh what a sight!

Straps of the Valiant

A brave little mouse wore a harness of pride,
As he ventured to seek out his dreams far and wide.
With cheese on his mind and a spring in his step,
His friends cheered him on, with plans full of pep!

He climbed up a hill, where the cats watched below,
And shouted, 'I'm coming, watch me steal the show!'
The cats started laughing, they thought it absurd,
That a mouse could outsmart them—it seemed quite unheard!

With a wiggle and jiggle, he dashed with great flair,
Triple backflips to chaos, he leapt through the air!
The straps held him tight, like they knew they must,
And the cats, oh, they laughed, 'We just can't adjust!'

So the mouse marched on, with a grin from ear to ear,
His courage not hidden, it blossomed with cheer.
For in the wild, on that bright sunny day,
He taught everyone how to laugh at their fray!

www.ingramcontent.com/pod-product-compliance
Lightning Source LLC
Chambersburg PA
CBHW062107280426
43661CB00086B/288